Hunting Crocodiles With
Steve Irwin

by Chip Lovitt

Contents

CELEBRATION PRESS
Pearson Learning Group

Capture That Croc!

The crocodile peers out over the water. Its dark eyes stare at the man on the shore. The croc is 12 feet long: a half-ton of muscle, tough scaly skin, and sharp teeth. Suddenly it sinks like a submarine. All the crocodile hunter can see is air bubbles on the surface.

It can be very dangerous to move a crocodile.

"This bloke is extremely dangerous," Steve Irwin tells his team. Steve is the crocodile hunter. His team moves with care and respect.

Ropes ready, Steve holds a piece of meat out over the water. The croc takes the bait. It jumps out of the water, jaws open. As the croc snaps, Steve's team throws a rope around the animal's top jaw. Then they throw another rope. The angry animal struggles wildly.

The team pulls the croc out of the water. Five men jump on it. One holds its head while Steve ropes its jaws shut.

The rest of the team joins in. Some grab the croc's midsection. Others hold on to its swinging tail. The team leader blindfolds the croc. The animal stops fighting for now.

It takes a dozen men and women to control this crocodile. Within minutes it's loaded into the back of Steve's truck. The croc is heading to a new, better home, but the wild ride is not over yet.

It takes 12 people to release the croc, too. Holding it tightly, they carry it to the water. Steve loosens the ropes and blindfold. On a signal, everyone lets go all at once. The croc dashes into the water on its short, powerful legs.

"Another successful capture and release, and he didn't lose a **scale**," Steve says.

Catching crocs is all in a day's work for Steve Irwin, known on television as "The Crocodile Hunter." The croc Steve just captured had grown too large for its pool at Steve's Australia Zoo and had to be moved to a new, larger one.

Steve Irwin and his team hold a crocodile carefully. They don't want to hurt it or themselves.

Steve Irwin is a **herpetologist**. He studies **reptiles**. Some people think that reptiles like crocodiles, lizards, and snakes are creepy. To Steve, though, they are beautiful animals that deserve our care and respect.

Meet Steve Irwin

Steve began his work with reptiles at a young age. When most kids turn six, their parents give them birthday gifts like bikes, toys, or games. Steve's mom and dad gave him exactly what he wanted: a 12-foot python snake!

Steve Irwin became interested in reptiles at a young age.

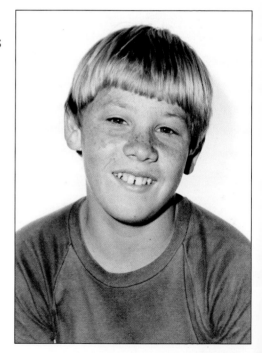

Young Steve often used his bare hands to catch crocodiles.

Steve Irwin was born in Victoria, Australia, in 1962. His parents, Bob and Lyn Irwin, founded an **animal refuge** called the Queensland Reptile and Fauna Park. Steve grew up around all kinds of animals.

Steve got a daily, hands-on education about animals, especially reptiles. He learned how to handle them and care for them. He studied their habits and moods.

Then the government asked Steve's father to move some dangerous crocs. He taught nine-year-old Steve to help him. They often caught freshwater crocodiles with their bare hands.

The animal refuge became home to nearly 100 crocodiles. It opened in 1973 and was later renamed Australia Zoo.

After high school Steve joined the government's crocodile **relocation** program. Its goal was to protect people and crocs by moving crocs away from areas where people lived, boated, or swam. Steve spent months searching rivers to capture **rogue crocodiles**.

Steve and Terri Irwin had their daughter, Bindi Sue, on July 24, 1998.

Steve met Terri Raines in 1991 when she visited Australia Zoo. Steve saw her in the crowd during one of his crocodile demonstrations.

"It was love at first sight," Steve says. They were married in Oregon in 1992.

Terri holds a light so they can film Steve and the croc.

On their wedding day, the couple got a call from a TV producer and friend, John Stainton, in Australia. Steve's help was needed to capture some crocs. John suggested they film the capture. That led to Steve's show, *The Crocodile Hunter*.

What a Crocodile!

Steve calls crocodiles "modern-day dinosaurs." With their thick, scaly skin, crocodiles do look like dinosaurs. Scientists think crocodile-like creatures may have existed 250 million years ago. Some may have been 50 feet long!

This prehistoric creature has a lot in common with modern-day crocodiles.

Today crocodiles can be found in tropical areas all over the world. They live in North and South America, Africa, Asia, and Australia, and are either **endangered**, protected, or nearly extinct. The smallest are about 4 feet long.

The largest are the saltwater crocodiles of Australia and Asia. "Salties" can grow up to 23 feet long and are the largest reptiles on Earth. Australian saltwater crocodiles have been known to attack humans. Their powerful jaws and huge teeth may frighten some people, but not Steve. He thinks they are amazing creatures that deserve our respect.

Most crocodiles are slow-moving. When angry or scared, though, some can move surprisingly fast. "Like greased lightning," says Steve. That's fast!

This crocodile is hard to see in the water.

A crocodile's eyes sit on top of its long, flat head. This makes it easy for the croc to hide. It can look out across the water while its body lies hidden under the water. It can see the crocodile hunter coming before he sees it.

Steve works hard to help save endangered crocs.

Crocodiles have been hunted for their meat and skin. Many lost their **habitats** when homes and farms were built nearby. Some were in danger of dying out. Laws have been passed to protect them. Steve is doing his part to help the crocs, too.

It's a Wild World

Steve's Australia Zoo is home to hundreds of animals: crocodiles, snakes, kangaroos, koalas, iguanas, tortoises, turtles, birds, and more. There are little lizards and big ones like the perentie, Australia's largest lizard, which grows more than 5 feet long.

The thorny devil is a type of lizard found in the Australian outback.

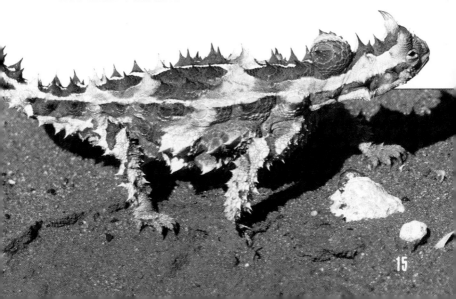

Zoo visitors can watch wildlife, see Steve feed the crocs, or hear **veterinarians** describe how hurt animals are cared for.

For Steve and Terri there's a world of animals outside the zoo, too. They search the world for animal rescues.

Visitors to Australia Zoo see how the crocodiles are fed.

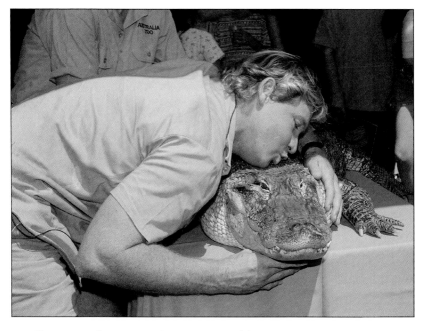

Steve *really* cares about crocodiles.

Steve and Terri helped save two sick crocodiles on an island in the Pacific Ocean. Steve and Terri built clean, roomy pens for them and taught the people there how to care for the island's crocodiles.

One of Steve's favorite places is Africa. He's filmed elephants, lions, snakes, crocs, and hippopotamuses there. He once visited Africa during the dry season. Rivers were drying up for lack of rain. Large herds of hippopotamuses and crocodiles had to share a smaller habitat. As he canoed down one river, Steve saw crocs and hippos fight for space.

This was a battle between two huge creatures. Hippos can grow more than 10 feet long and can weigh more than 5,000 pounds. It wasn't the most amazing sight Steve saw that day, though.

Farther down the river he saw dozens of crocodiles fighting over a dead hippo they had found. The crocodiles thrashed against each other. Steve thought it looked like dinosaurs fighting.

Big crocs don't scare Steve. He thinks they are awesome.

For Steve, being so close to fighting crocs proved a point. He didn't feel threatened by the crocs. "Millions of people in Africa share the territory of this magnificent **species** every single day," he says.

Risky Business

Wildlife **documentaries** used to be filmed from a distance. Now they are often filmed close up, using fixed and hand-held cameras. Steve likes to get right next to the animals when he films. That can be dangerous.

This snake is only inches away from Steve's face.

In his work Steve has to get very close to wildlife.

Steve has been chased by a cheetah, kicked by a kangaroo, and pecked at by an **emu**. He's dived with sharks, tangled with tarantulas, and been bitten by pythons. A Komodo dragon once chased him up a tree.

Steve handles all kinds of snakes.

Steve has handled the world's most dangerous snakes, from **venomous** red-bellied black snakes to 12-foot black mambas. "I've never had a real serious bite from any animal," he said. "I have never been bitten by a venomous snake."

Steve's adventures have won him millions of fans. Yet some say he is more of a showman than a scientist. Others claim he's more interested in being a star than in education.

He disagrees. "Terri and I eat, sleep, and live for wildlife," he says. Steve has great love for animals and wants to make sure they live on.

At the zoo he saves endangered species and cares for hurt animals on a 250-acre conservation area. He shares his knowledge of wildlife with visitors. His TV show teaches people about endangered animals and how to save them.

"I'm a thrill seeker," Steve also admits. "But crikey!" he says, using his favorite expression. "Education's the most important thing."

Glossary

animal refuge	a place of safety for hurt or endangered animals
documentary	a film that shows real-life events, people, places, or animals
emu	a large, ostrich-like bird
endangered	at risk of dying out and becoming extinct
habitat	the place where an animal or plant lives
herpetologist	someone who studies reptiles
relocation	moving something from one place to another
reptile	a coldblooded animal that has a backbone and scales, breathes air, and crawls on its belly or short legs
rogue crocodile	a crocodile that has to be moved to places where people do not live
scale	a thin, flat, hard plate that covers certain fish and reptiles
species	a group of animals or plants that share common traits
venomous	poisonous
veterinarian	an animal doctor